WELCOME TO THE U.S.A.
NORTH CAROLINA

Written by Ann Heinrichs   Illustrated by Matt Kania
Content Adviser: Michael Hill, Research Supervisor, North Carolina
Office of Archives and History, Raleigh, North Carolina

Published in the United States of America by The Child's World®
PO Box 326 • Chanhassen, MN 55317-0326
800-599-READ • www.childsworld.com

Photo Credits
Cover: NC Division of Tourism, Film, and Sports Development; frontispiece: NC Division of Tourism, Film, and Sports Development.

Interior: Corbis: 10 (Richard T. Nowtiz), 11 (Raymond Gehman), 25 (Richard A. Cooke); Discovery Place: 29; Getty Images: 17 (Stone/Charles Gupton), 23 (CBS Photo Archive), 33 (Craig Jones); High Point Convention & Visitors Bureau: 18; JAARS/Museum of the Alphabet: 34; Library of Congress: 27; NC Division of Tourism, Film, and Sports Development: 6, 9, 13, 14, 21, 22, 30; Photodisc: 26.

Acknowledgments
The Child's World®: Mary Berendes, Publishing Director

Editorial Directions, Inc.: E. Russell Primm, Editorial Director; Katie Marsico, Associate Editor; Judith Shiffer, Assistant Editor; Matt Messbarger, Editorial Assistant; Susan Hindman, Copy Editor; Melissa McDaniel, Proofreader; Peter Garnham, Matt Messbarger, Olivia Nellums, Chris Simms, Molly Symmonds, Katherine Trickle, Carl Stephen Wender, Fact Checkers; Tim Griffin/IndexServ, Indexer; Cian Loughlin O'Day, Photo Researcher and Editor

The Design Lab: Kathleen Petelinsek, design and art production

Library of Congress Cataloging-in-Publication Data
Heinrichs, Ann.
  North Carolina / written by Ann Heinrichs ; cartography and illustrations by Matt Kania.
    p. cm. — (Welcome to the U.S.A.)
  Includes index.
  ISBN 1-59296-287-4 (lib. bdg. : alk. paper) 1. North Carolina—Juvenile literature. 2. North Carolina—Geography—Juvenile literature. I. Kania, Matt. II. Title. III. Series.
  F254.3.H453 2005
  975.6—dc22   2004005714

Ann Heinrichs is the author of more than 100 books for children and young adults. She has also enjoyed successful careers as a children's book editor and an advertising copywriter. Ann grew up in Fort Smith, Arkansas, and lives in Chicago, Illinois.

About the Author Ann Heinrichs

Matt Kania loves maps and, as a kid, dreamed of making them. In school he studied geography and cartography, and today he makes maps for a living. Matt's favorite thing about drawing maps is learning about the places they represent. Many of the maps he has created can be found in books, magazines, videos, Web sites, and public places.

About the Map Illustrator Matt Kania

On the cover: Do you enjoy kayaking? Take a ride on North Carolina's Nantahala River!
On page one: This lighthouse is located on Bodie Island.

OUR NORTH CAROLINA TRIP

North Carolina's Nicknames: The Tar Heel State and the Old North State

What will you do in North Carolina today? Meet Andy Griffith and the Wright brothers? See black bears and talking trees? Get the scoop on pirates and race cars? Why not do it all? Just buckle up and start your engines! Follow the dotted line and hang on tight. You're on the fast track to fun!

WELCOME TO NORTH CAROLINA

As you travel through North Carolina, watch for all the interesting facts along the way.

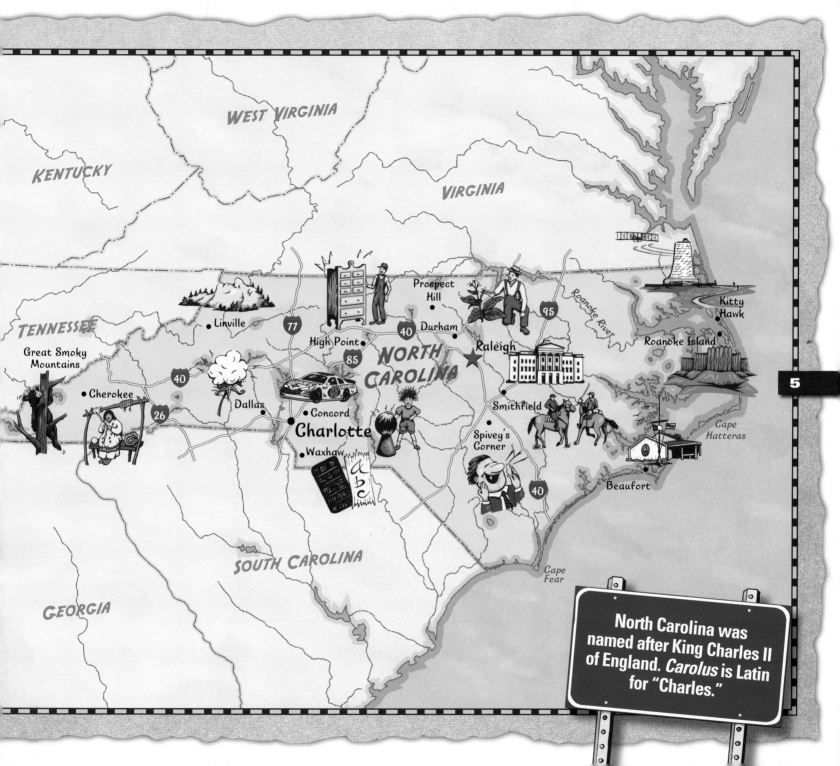

KENTUCKY

WEST VIRGINIA

VIRGINIA

TENNESSEE

Great Smoky
Mountains

Cherokee

Linville

77

High Point

40

Durham

Prospect
Hill

NORTH
CAROLINA

Roanoke River

Kitty
Hawk

Roanoke Island

85

Raleigh

Dallas

Concord

Charlotte

Smithfield

Waxhaw

Spivey's
Corner

40

Beaufort

Cape
Hatteras

SOUTH CAROLINA

Cape
Fear

26

40

95

GEORGIA

5

North Carolina was
named after King Charles II
of England. *Carolus* is Latin
for "Charles."

Do you want adventure on the high seas?
Visit the North Carolina Maritime Museum.

The shoals—areas of shallow, shifting sandbars—are called the Graveyard of the Atlantic. Many ships have sunk in their shallow waters.

Blackbeard was a fierce pirate. People trembled when they heard his name! His ship *Queen Anne's Revenge* sank in 1718. Historians believe they've found it. Just visit the North Carolina Maritime Museum in Beaufort. It displays objects from the ship.

North Carolina faces the Atlantic Ocean. Long, sandy islands called sandbars lie offshore. They reach up to 15 miles (24 kilometers) out into the ocean.

Mountains cover western North Carolina. The Blue Ridge Mountains are the biggest range. The Great Smoky Mountains rise there, too. They belong to the Appalachian Mountain Range. Central North Carolina is hilly. Rivers run from there to the coast.

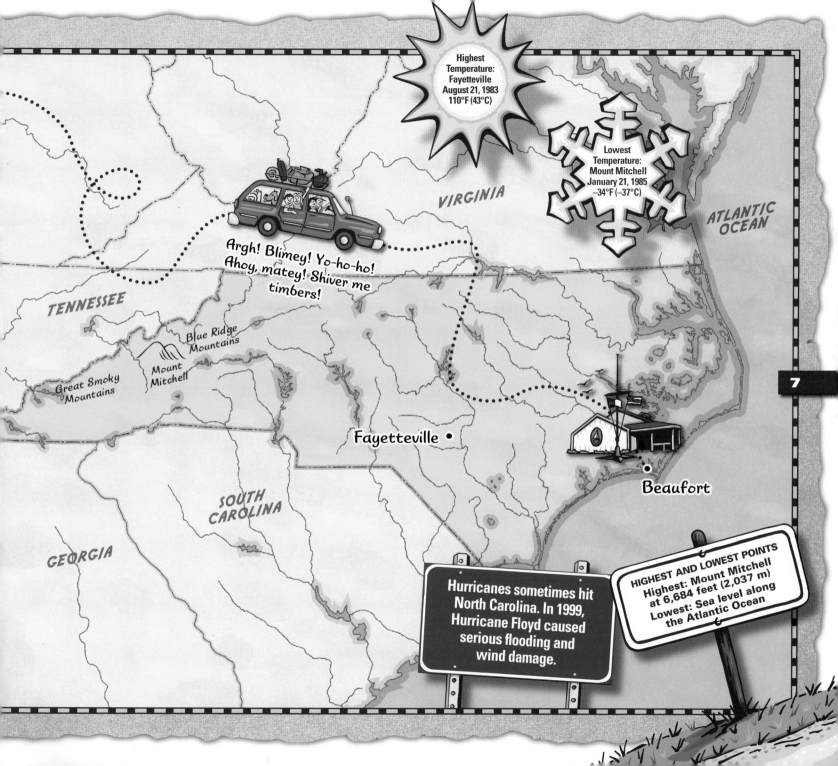

Highest Temperature: Fayetteville August 21, 1983 110°F (43°C)

Lowest Temperature: Mount Mitchell January 21, 1985 −34°F (−37°C)

VIRGINIA

ATLANTIC OCEAN

Argh! Blimey! Yo-ho-ho! Ahoy, matey! Shiver me timbers!

TENNESSEE

Blue Ridge Mountains

Mount Mitchell

Great Smoky Mountains

Fayetteville •

Beaufort

SOUTH CAROLINA

GEORGIA

Hurricanes sometimes hit North Carolina. In 1999, Hurricane Floyd caused serious flooding and wind damage.

HIGHEST AND LOWEST POINTS
Highest: Mount Mitchell at 6,684 feet (2,037 m)
Lowest: Sea level along the Atlantic Ocean

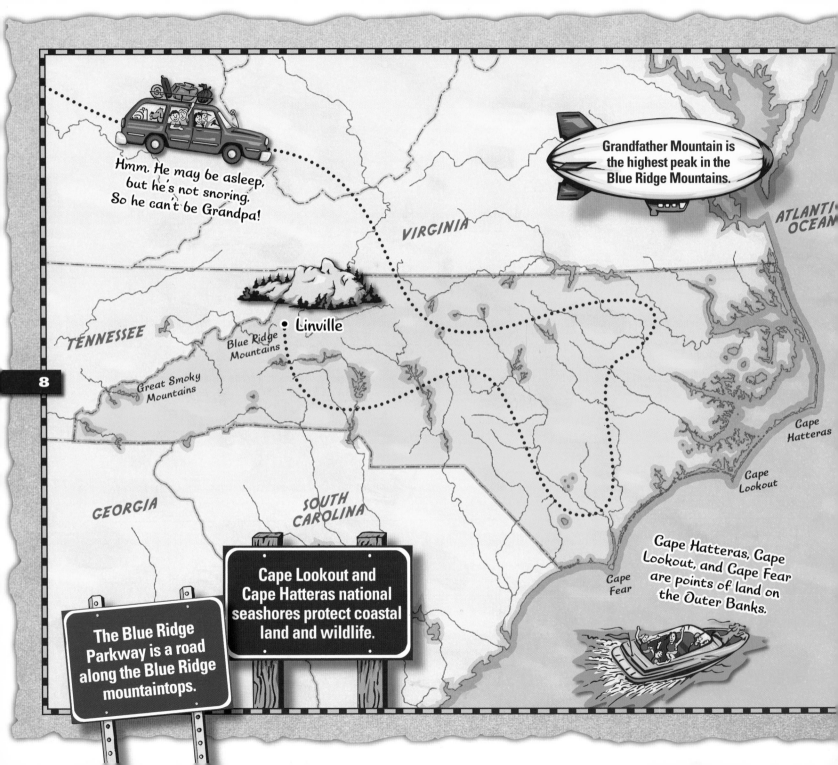

8

Grandfather Mountain is the highest peak in the Blue Ridge Mountains.

ATLANTIC OCEAN

Hmm. He may be asleep, but he's not snoring. So he can't be Grandpa!

VIRGINIA

TENNESSEE

• Linville

Blue Ridge Mountains

Great Smoky Mountains

Cape Hatteras

Cape Lookout

GEORGIA

SOUTH CAROLINA

Cape Fear

Cape Hatteras, Cape Lookout, and Cape Fear are points of land on the Outer Banks.

Cape Lookout and Cape Hatteras national seashores protect coastal land and wildlife.

The Blue Ridge Parkway is a road along the Blue Ridge mountaintops.

Grandfather Mountain and the Blue Ridge Parkway

He looks old. And he looks like he's asleep. This rocky face is Grandfather Mountain. It "sleeps" in Linville along the Blue Ridge Parkway.

You'll love roaming the Blue Ridge Mountains. They rise along North Carolina's border with Virginia. You can hike or ride bikes for miles. You might even see deer and black bears. Or try the Smoky Mountains. You can ride a train through the valleys.

The coast is another fun place. There you'll gather seashells and visit **lighthouses.** Look out at the rocky banks. You'll see why so many ships crashed there!

All aboard! Hop on a railroad train to view the scenic Smoky Mountains.

Cape Hatteras is home to the tallest lighthouse in the United States.

Once I lost a toy. Once I lost my cat. But North Carolina lost a whole colony!

North Carolina's first European settlers sailed from England. They arrived at Roanoke Island in 1585. There they set up Fort Raleigh. Life was hard in their new land. The settlers soon returned to England.

Another group came in 1587. Three years later, they were gone. There were 116 men, women, and children in all. No one knows what happened. They simply disappeared. This is called the Lost **Colony.**

More settlers arrived. They set up the Carolina Colony. It split into two colonies in 1712. They were named North Carolina and South Carolina.

The story of the Lost Colony became a play. It's performed on Roanoke Island.

North Carolina was among the 13 original colonies. The colonies gained freedom from British rule in the American Revolution (1775–1783).

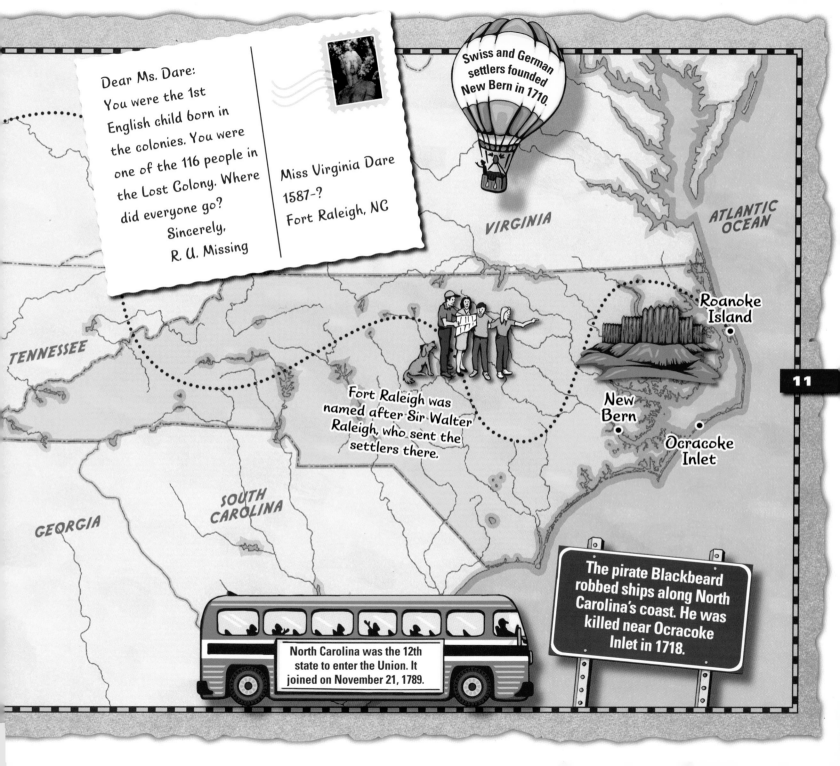

Dear Ms. Dare:
You were the 1st English child born in the colonies. You were one of the 116 people in the Lost Colony. Where did everyone go?
Sincerely,
R. U. Missing

Miss Virginia Dare
1587-?
Fort Raleigh, NC

Swiss and German settlers founded New Bern in 1710.

VIRGINIA

ATLANTIC OCEAN

TENNESSEE

Fort Raleigh was named after Sir Walter Raleigh, who sent the settlers there.

Roanoke Island

New Bern

Ocracoke Inlet

SOUTH CAROLINA

GEORGIA

North Carolina was the 12th state to enter the Union. It joined on November 21, 1789.

The pirate Blackbeard robbed ships along North Carolina's coast. He was killed near Ocracoke Inlet in 1718.

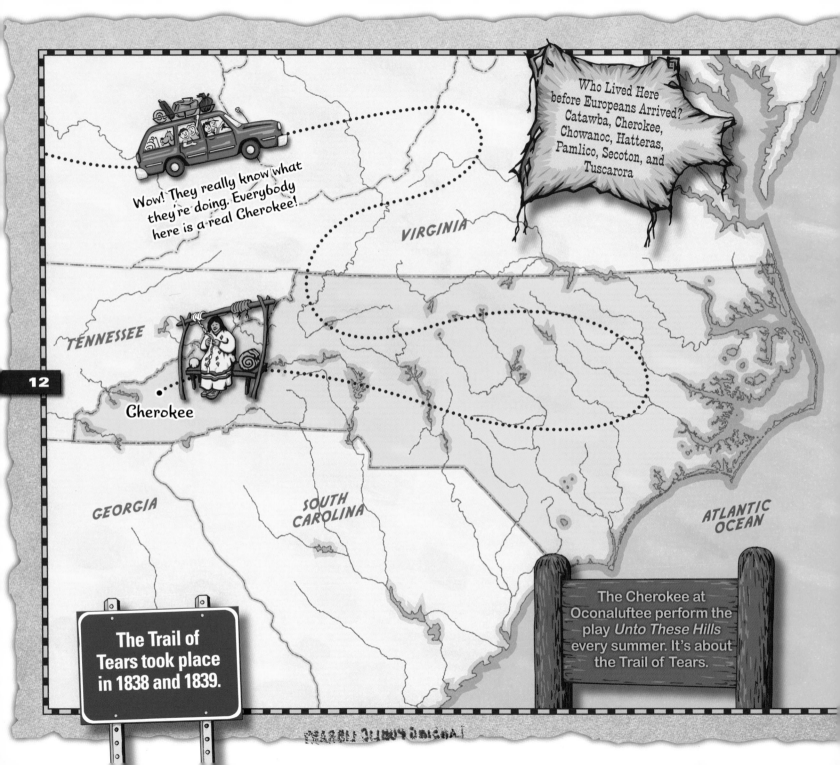

Wow! They really know what they're doing. Everybody here is a real Cherokee!

Who Lived Here before Europeans Arrived? Catawba, Cherokee, Chowanoc, Hatteras, Pamlico, Secoton, and Tuscarora

VIRGINIA

TENNESSEE

Cherokee

GEORGIA

SOUTH CAROLINA

ATLANTIC OCEAN

The Trail of Tears took place in 1838 and 1839.

The Cherokee at Oconaluftee perform the play *Unto These Hills* every summer. It's about the Trail of Tears.

C link, clink! There's a nice, pointy arrowhead. Fwit! There goes a **blowgun** dart. You've stepped back to the 1750s. You're in a Cherokee village. Everywhere you look, people are busy with crafts. It's Oconaluftee Indian Village in Cherokee.

Thousands of American Indians once lived in North Carolina. They hunted, fished, and grew crops. They made everything they needed.

In the 1830s, the Cherokee were driven out. They were sent to present-day Oklahoma. It was called Indian Territory at the time. Thousands died along the way. This journey is called the Trail of Tears.

Actors in Cherokee perform *Unto These Hills.*

13

Dig in! Watch your flank! Hold that line! Close that gap!

Horsemen are attacking! Foot soldiers are on the move! And here come the big cannons! It's Bentonville Battlefield. People act out this battle every year.

Slavery was common in the South. Slaves worked on North Carolina's plantations. These huge farms grew cotton and tobacco. But many people in the Northern states opposed slavery. The two sides broke apart. They fought the Civil War (1861–1865).

North Carolina joined the South, or Confederates. The Battle of Bentonville took place near Smithfield. Confederates lost this battle and the war, too. Then the slaves were freed.

Are you back in the 1800s? No, you're just watching costumed actors at Bentonville.

14

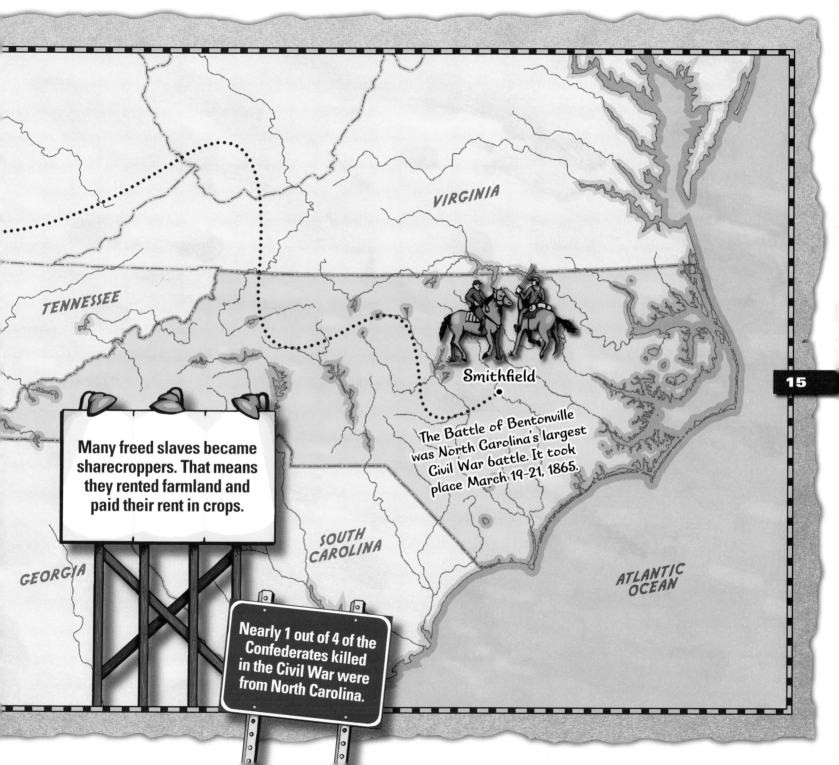

VIRGINIA

TENNESSEE

Smithfield

The Battle of Bentonville was North Carolina's largest Civil War battle. It took place March 19-21, 1865.

Many freed slaves became sharecroppers. That means they rented farmland and paid their rent in crops.

SOUTH CAROLINA

GEORGIA

Nearly 1 out of 4 of the Confederates killed in the Civil War were from North Carolina.

ATLANTIC OCEAN

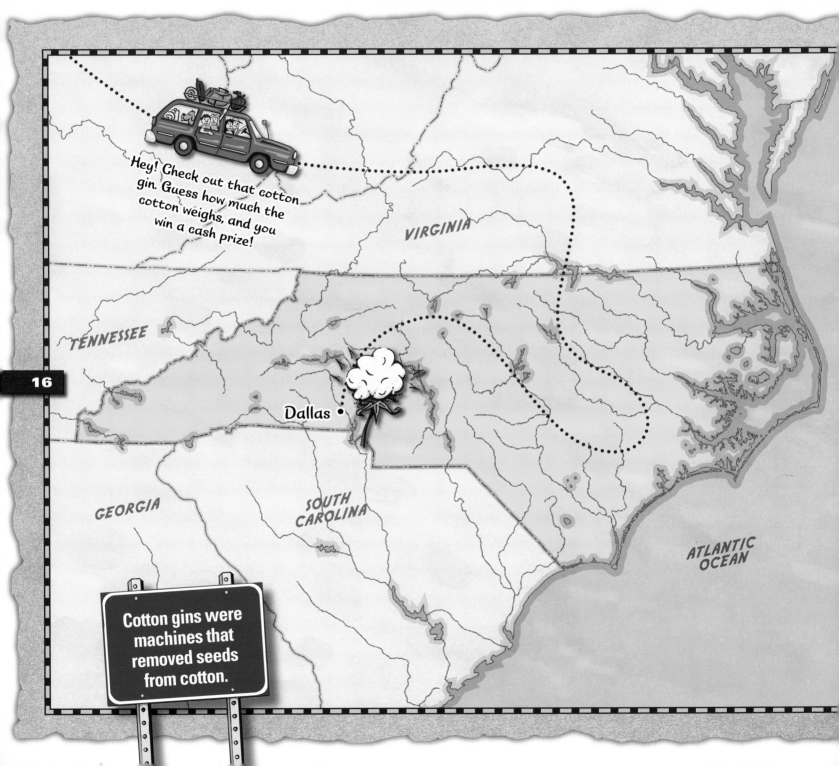

Hey! Check out that cotton gin. Guess how much the cotton weighs, and you win a cash prize!

VIRGINIA

TENNESSEE

16

Dallas

GEORGIA

SOUTH CAROLINA

ATLANTIC OCEAN

Cotton gins were machines that removed seeds from cotton.

Cotton Ginning Days in Dallas

Chug, chug. Sputter, sputter. Crank up those creaky old tractors. It's Cotton Ginning Days in Dallas! These old farm machines are the stars. They're more than 100 years old!

This festival celebrates North Carolina's farming history. Farming led the way to some large **industries.** Cotton mills made cotton cloth. Factories turned tobacco into smoking products.

Trees were useful, too. Sawmills cut up the logs. Then factories made wooden furniture. All these products made money for the state. No more chugging and sputtering! Those factories buzzed and whirred!

Does this wood look familiar? Maybe it was used to make your living room furniture!

Listen! That tree is talking! Is this an enchanted forest?

Harvey Hardwood is a friendly guy. He tells you all about wood and furniture. Actually, he's not a guy. He's a talking tree! He's at the Furniture Discovery Center in High Point.

This center is a great place to explore. You'll learn about different kinds of wood. You'll learn how furniture is made. You'll see fifteen tiny, hand-carved bedrooms. And you'll meet Harvey!

North Carolina is the top state for wooden furniture. It's also the top state for textiles, or cloth. Put them together, and what have you got? A sofa!

Harvey Hardwood weighs 500 pounds (227 kg). He's made of solid red oak.

18

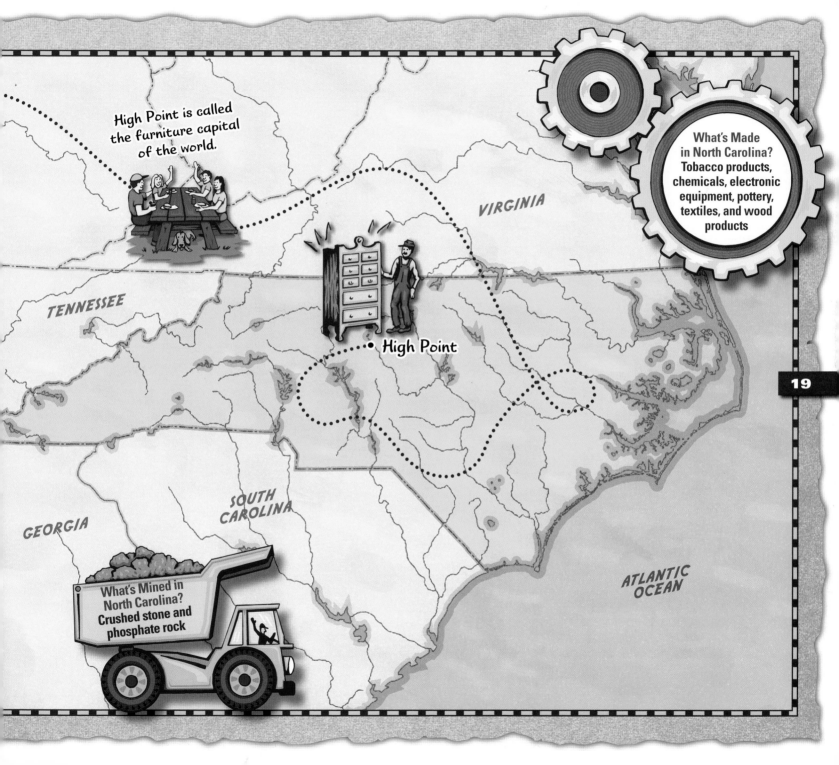

High Point is called the furniture capital of the world.

VIRGINIA

TENNESSEE

• High Point

GEORGIA

SOUTH CAROLINA

ATLANTIC OCEAN

What's Made in North Carolina? Tobacco products, chemicals, electronic equipment, pottery, textiles, and wood products

What's Mined in North Carolina? Crushed stone and phosphate rock

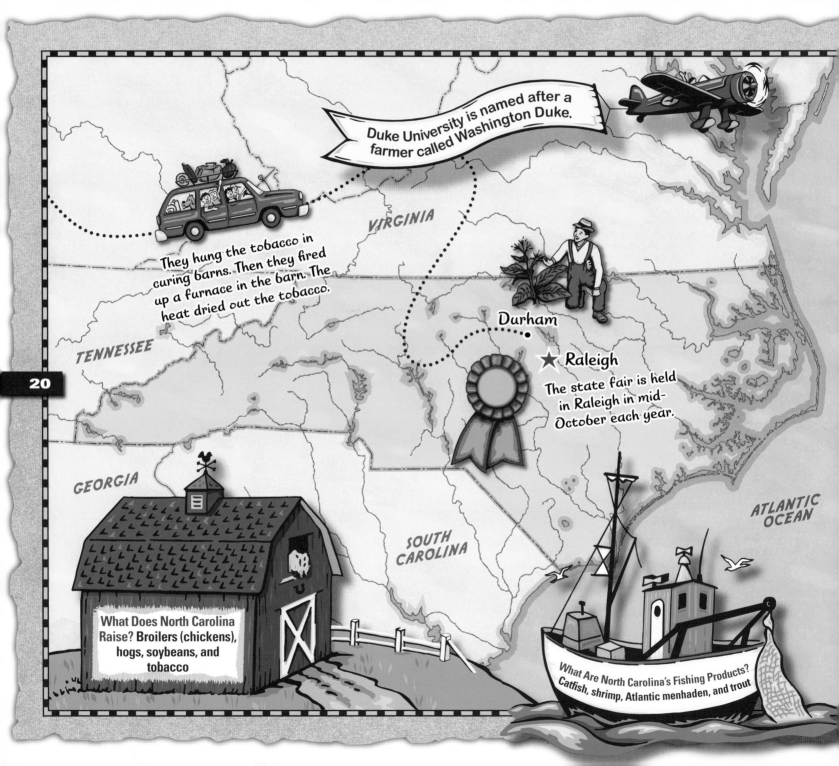

Duke University is named after a farmer called Washington Duke.

They hung the tobacco in curing barns. Then they fired up a furnace in the barn. The heat dried out the tobacco.

VIRGINIA

TENNESSEE

Durham

★ Raleigh

The state fair is held in Raleigh in mid-October each year.

GEORGIA

SOUTH CAROLINA

ATLANTIC OCEAN

What Does North Carolina Raise? Broilers (chickens), hogs, soybeans, and tobacco

What Are North Carolina's Fishing Products? Catfish, shrimp, Atlantic menhaden, and trout

Top it, sucker it, and worm it? What does all that mean? Well, it was pretty hard work. That's what tobacco farmers did to their plants. Just check out Duke Homestead and Tobacco Museum. It was a big tobacco farm in the 1800s. It also had one of the first tobacco factories. You'll see how tobacco was grown and processed.

A farmer harvests tobacco at Duke Homestead.

North Carolina is the leading tobacco state. Farmers started growing tobacco in the 1700s. Corn and peanuts are important crops, too. And don't forget the animals. Lots of North Carolina farmers raise chickens, hogs, and turkeys.

21

Topping means removing the top of the plant to control growth. Suckering is removing new shoots. Worming means keeping pests away.

Where are those earplugs?
What? I can't hear you.

Want to dance? Just visit the Ole Time
Fiddler's and Bluegrass Festival.

Actor Andy
Griffith was born
in Mount Airy.

The National Hollerin' Contest in Spivey's Corner

Eeee-OO! Yo-AH-dee-oh! What's all that yelling about? You've stumbled into the National Hollerin' Contest!

This contest is held in Spivey's Corner every summer. It celebrates an old-time folk custom—hollerin'! Country folks used to yell across the fields. They'd greet neighbors or call for help. They'd announce dinner time or call in the pigs. There was always something to holler about!

North Carolina has many folk **traditions.** Union Grove celebrates old music. It holds the Ole Time Fiddler's and Bluegrass Festival. Asheville presents the Mountain Dance and Folk Festival. You're bound to hear some hollerin' there!

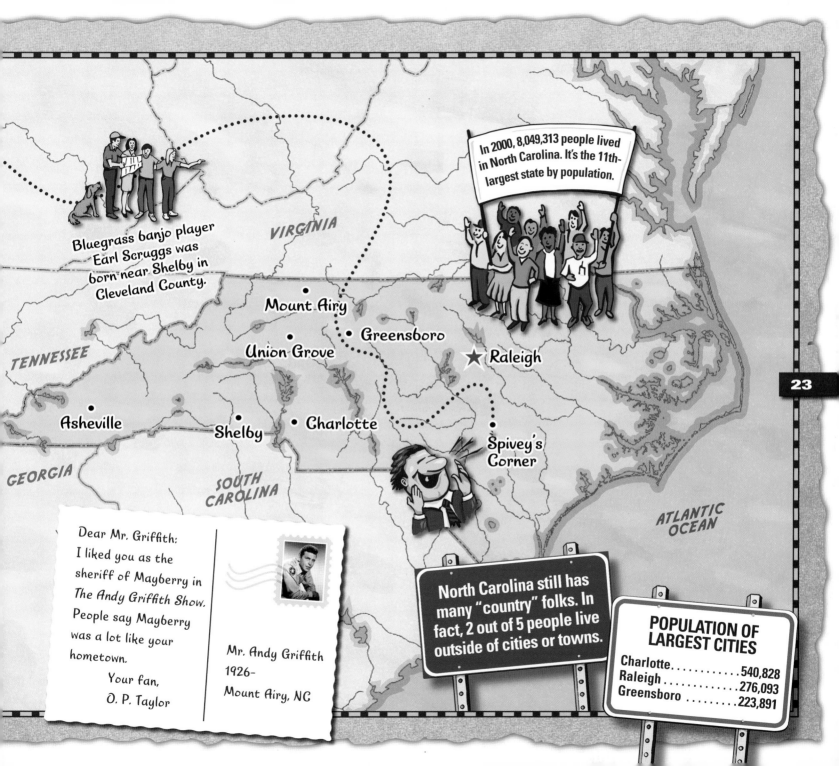

Bluegrass banjo player Earl Scruggs was born near Shelby in Cleveland County.

VIRGINIA

In 2000, 8,049,313 people lived in North Carolina. It's the 11th-largest state by population.

TENNESSEE

Mount Airy

• Greensboro

Union Grove

★ Raleigh

Asheville

Shelby • Charlotte

Spivey's Corner

GEORGIA

SOUTH CAROLINA

ATLANTIC OCEAN

Dear Mr. Griffith:
I liked you as the sheriff of Mayberry in The Andy Griffith Show. People say Mayberry was a lot like your hometown.

Your fan,
O. P. Taylor

Mr. Andy Griffith
1926-
Mount Airy, NC

North Carolina still has many "country" folks. In fact, 2 out of 5 people live outside of cities or towns.

POPULATION OF LARGEST CITIES

Charlotte 540,828
Raleigh 276,093
Greensboro 223,891

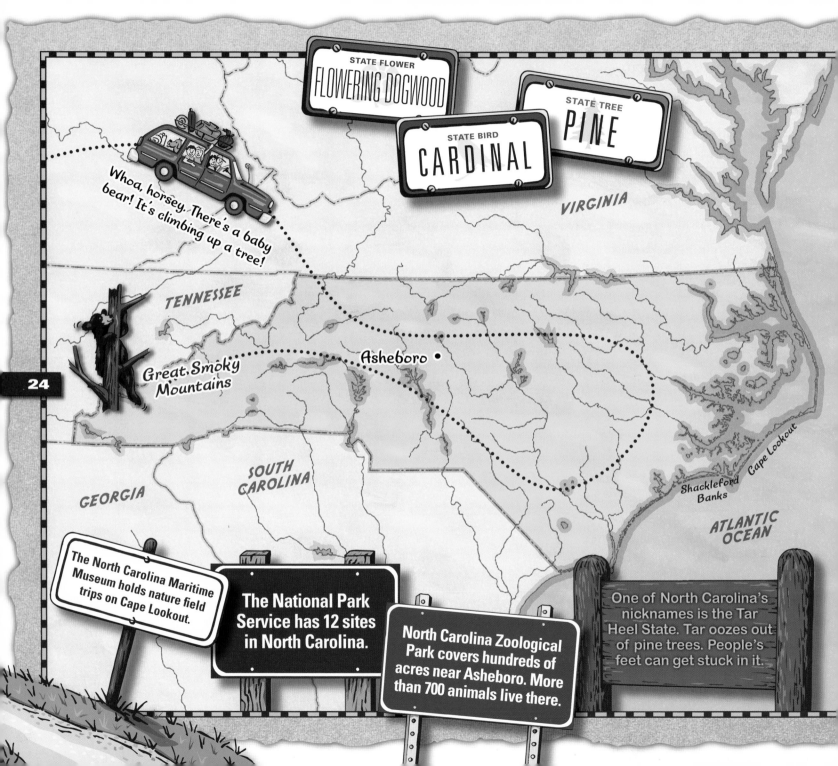

STATE FLOWER
FLOWERING DOGWOOD

STATE BIRD
CARDINAL

STATE TREE
PINE

VIRGINIA

Whoa, horsey. There's a baby bear! It's climbing up a tree!

TENNESSEE

Great Smoky Mountains

Asheboro •

SOUTH CAROLINA

GEORGIA

Shackleford Banks

Cape Lookout

ATLANTIC OCEAN

24

The North Carolina Maritime Museum holds nature field trips on Cape Lookout.

The National Park Service has 12 sites in North Carolina.

North Carolina Zoological Park covers hundreds of acres near Asheboro. More than 700 animals live there.

One of North Carolina's nicknames is the Tar Heel State. Tar oozes out of pine trees. People's feet can get stuck in it.

Critters in the Great Smoky Mountains

Take a horseback ride through the Great Smoky Mountains. You'll run into all kinds of critters. The most famous **resident** is the black bear. About 1,800 of them live in the Smokies. The baby bears are really cute!

Chipmunks and deer live in the Smokies, too. So do wolves and mountain lions. They hide in the deep forests. Much of North Carolina is covered with forests.

Crabs live along the coast. Sea turtles nest there, too. You might even see some bears near the coast. Offshore, you'll see dolphins and sailfish.

Watch out! Black bears live in the Smokies. They're cute, but don't get too close!

Wild horses roam on Shackleford Banks. This island is on the Outer Banks.

Are the winds too rough? Will my kite stay up longer than the Wright brothers did? Will it crash?

It's off! It glides. It soars. And finally, it scoots down into the sand. You're at Kitty Hawk on kite-flying day! Today, it's only your kite. But in 1903, it was a famous airplane. The Wright brothers flew the first engine-powered aircraft here. Their names were Orville and Wilbur. They're called the fathers of **aviation.**

The Wrights' first flight lasted only twelve seconds. They tried three more times. The last flight lasted fifty-nine seconds. It was shaky, but it was a start. This led the way to high-speed flight— and space travel!

A monument at Kitty Hawk honors the Wright Brothers.

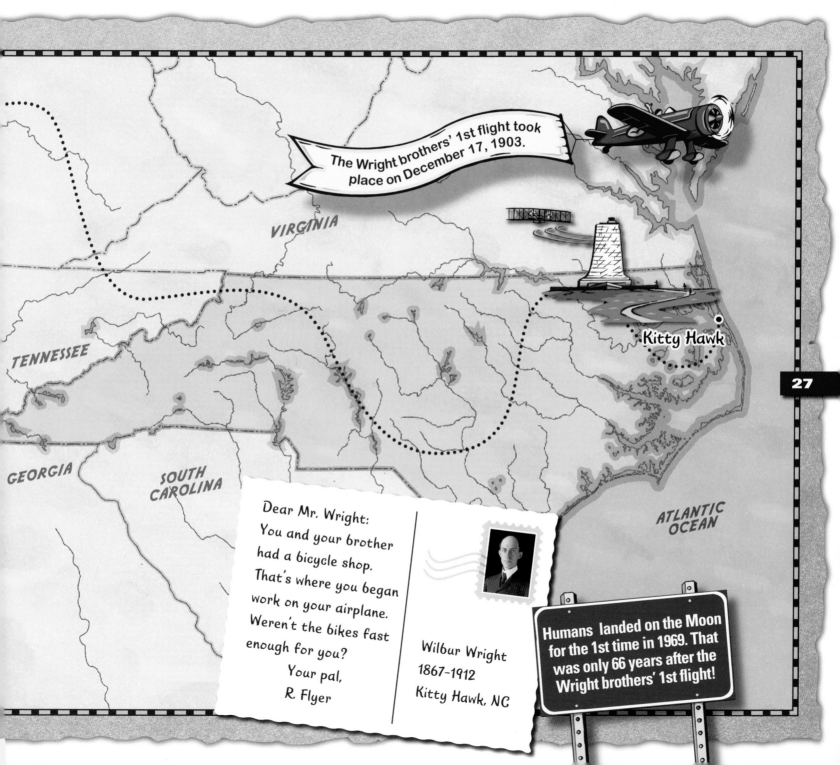

The Wright brothers' 1st flight took place on December 17, 1903.

VIRGINIA

TENNESSEE

GEORGIA

SOUTH CAROLINA

Kitty Hawk

ATLANTIC OCEAN

Dear Mr. Wright:
You and your brother had a bicycle shop. That's where you began work on your airplane. Weren't the bikes fast enough for you?
Your pal,
R. Flyer

Wilbur Wright
1867-1912
Kitty Hawk, NC

Humans landed on the Moon for the 1st time in 1969. That was only 66 years after the Wright brothers' 1st flight!

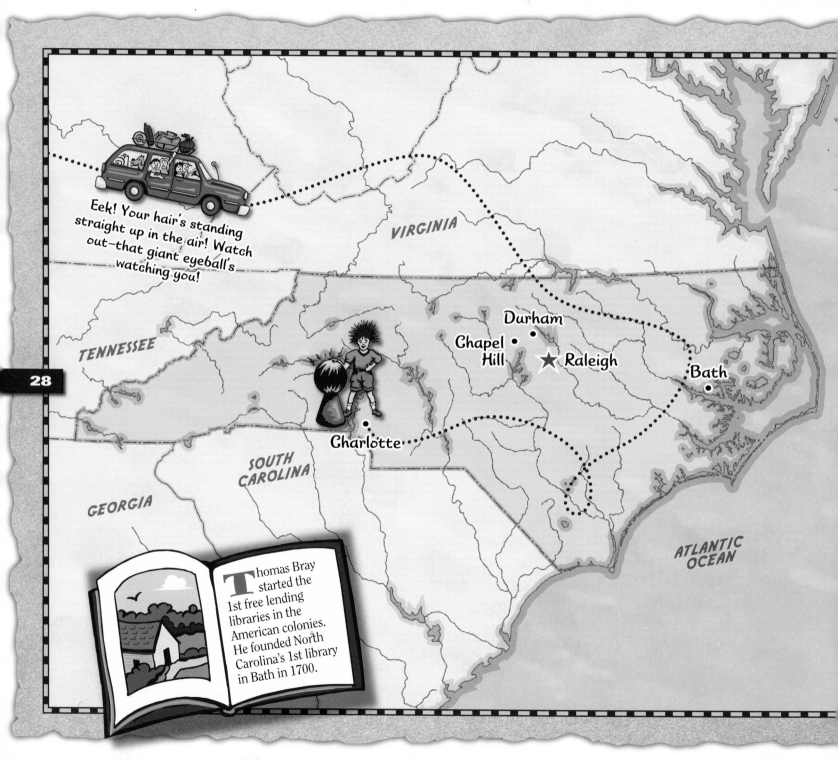

Eek! Your hair's standing straight up in the air! Watch out—that giant eyeball's watching you!

VIRGINIA

TENNESSEE

Durham

Chapel Hill

★ Raleigh

Bath

Charlotte

SOUTH CAROLINA

GEORGIA

ATLANTIC OCEAN

Thomas Bray started the 1st free lending libraries in the American colonies. He founded North Carolina's 1st library in Bath in 1700.

Looking for a fun place to learn about science? Try Discovery Place. It's a science museum in Charlotte. One exhibit is a giant eyeball. You can walk inside it! Another exhibit zaps you with **static electricity.** It makes your hair stand on end!

Science is a big deal in North Carolina. Three universities lead the way. One is North Carolina State University in Raleigh. Another is the University of North Carolina at Chapel Hill. The third is Duke University in Durham.

These universities helped open a business and research center in 1959. It's called Research Triangle Park. Scientists there find new ways to make better products.

This visitor is learning about electricity at Discovery Place.

29

If you drew lines to connect the 3 universities, they would make a triangle, or 3-sided figure.

The state capitol in Raleigh was completed in 1840.

Welcome to Raleigh, the capital of North Carolina!

s it a museum? Is it an office building? It's both! It's the state capitol in Raleigh. Some state government offices are inside. But mostly this three-story building is a museum. You'll see lots of fancy rooms with high ceilings. Some were once meeting rooms for lawmakers. One used to be the state library. And one held a big rock collection!

North Carolina's government has three branches. One branch carries out the laws. Its offices are in the capitol. The governor heads this branch. Another branch makes the laws. It's called the General Assembly. Courts make up the third branch. They decide whether laws have been broken.

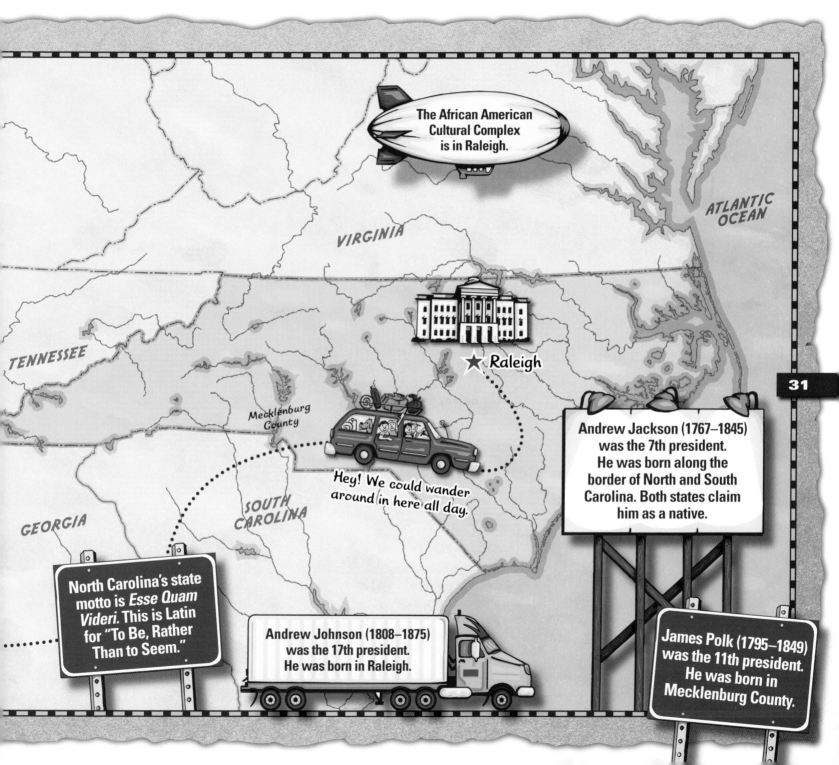

The African American Cultural Complex is in Raleigh.

ATLANTIC OCEAN

VIRGINIA

TENNESSEE

★ Raleigh

Mecklenburg County

Hey! We could wander around in here all day.

SOUTH CAROLINA

GEORGIA

Andrew Jackson (1767–1845) was the 7th president. He was born along the border of North and South Carolina. Both states claim him as a native.

North Carolina's state motto is *Esse Quam Videri*. This is Latin for "To Be, Rather Than to Seem."

Andrew Johnson (1808–1875) was the 17th president. He was born in Raleigh.

James Polk (1795–1849) was the 11th president. He was born in Mecklenburg County.

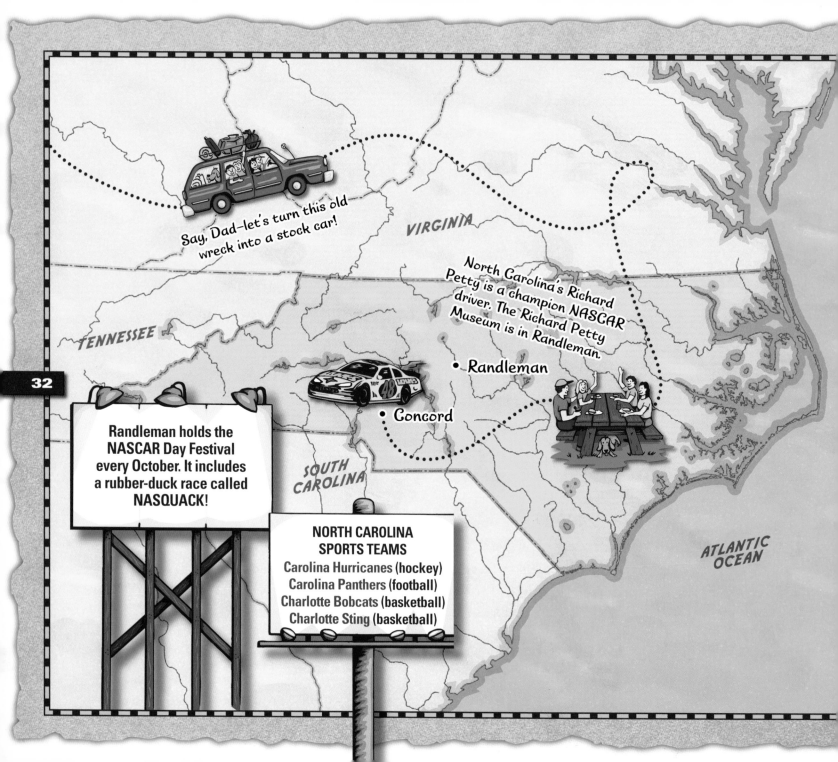

Say, Dad—let's turn this old wreck into a stock car!

VIRGINIA

North Carolina's Richard Petty is a champion NASCAR driver. The Richard Petty Museum is in Randleman.

TENNESSEE

• Randleman

• Concord

Randleman holds the NASCAR Day Festival every October. It includes a rubber-duck race called NASQUACK!

SOUTH CAROLINA

NORTH CAROLINA SPORTS TEAMS
Carolina Hurricanes (hockey)
Carolina Panthers (football)
Charlotte Bobcats (basketball)
Charlotte Sting (basketball)

ATLANTIC OCEAN

Lowe's Motor Speedway in Concord

Vroom! Take a spin around the racetrack. See the pits where the cars gas up. You're touring Lowe's Motor Speedway in Concord!

North Carolina is wild about car racing. It's got dozens of race tracks! Lowe's is a popular track. It holds lots of exciting NASCAR races. Those are races for stock cars. They're regular cars—just like the ones you ride. Only they've been fixed up so they go "Vroom!"

Start your engines! You're at the NASCAR races in Concord.

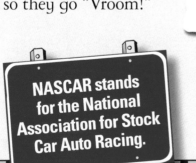

NASCAR stands for the National Association for Stock Car Auto Racing.

Alpha, beta, gamma . . . this is too hard. I think I'll invent my own alphabet.

Okay. You're a pretty good reader. And your spelling's pretty good, too. But what are α and β and ΩΠΣ? Don't know? Sorry! No spelling bee prize for you today!

You're at the Museum of the Alphabet in Waxhaw. It tells all about the history of writing. You'll learn about dozens of alphabets there. And you'll learn about the people who invented them.

What about the strange letters above? They're Greek. Start studying!

34

You probably know your ABCs. But you'll learn about different alphabets in Waxhaw.

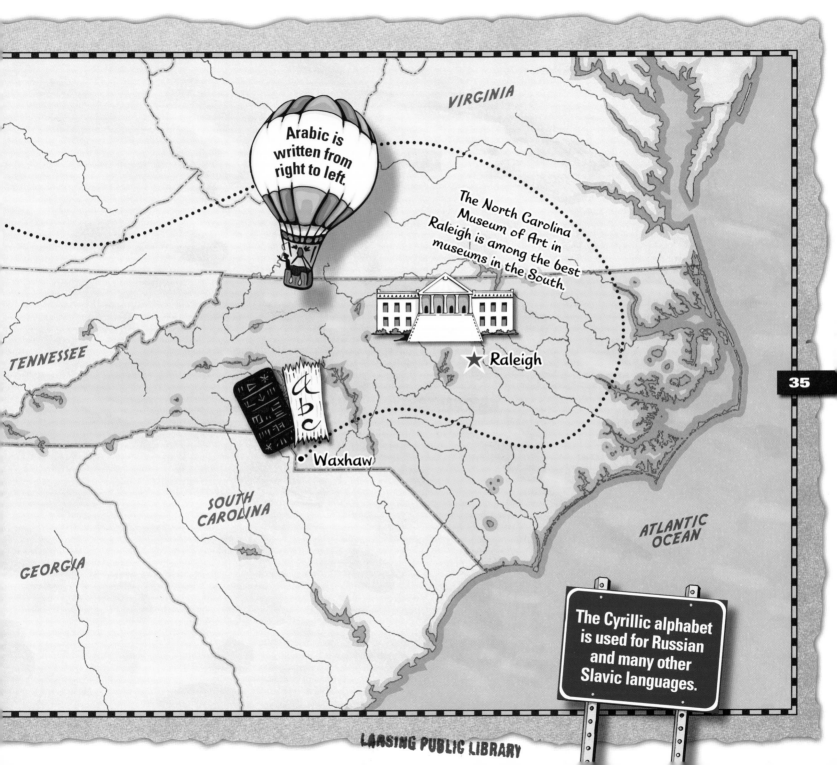

VIRGINIA

Arabic is written from right to left.

The North Carolina Museum of Art in Raleigh is among the best museums in the South.

★ Raleigh

TENNESSEE

• Waxhaw

SOUTH CAROLINA

GEORGIA

ATLANTIC OCEAN

The Cyrillic alphabet is used for Russian and many other Slavic languages.

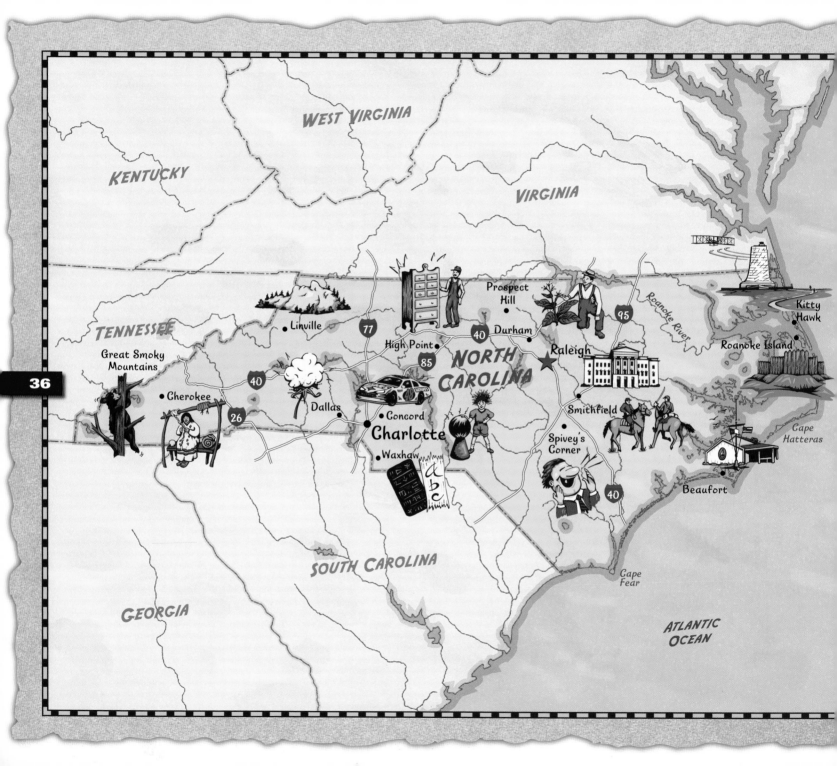

KENTUCKY

WEST VIRGINIA

VIRGINIA

TENNESSEE

Linville

Great Smoky
Mountains

Cherokee

Dallas

77

High Point

85

40

Durham

NORTH
CAROLINA

Raleigh

Prospect
Hill

95

Roanoke River

Kitty
Hawk

Roanoke Island

Concord

Charlotte

Waxhaw

40

26

Smithfield

Spivey's
Corner

40

Beaufort

Cape
Hatteras

SOUTH CAROLINA

Cape
Fear

GEORGIA

ATLANTIC
OCEAN

OUR TRIP

We visited many amazing places on our trip! We also met a lot of interesting people along the way. Look at the map on the left. Use your finger to trace all the places we have been.

Who is North Carolina named after? See page 5 for the answer.

Where is the tallest lighthouse in the United States? Page 9 has the answer.

What was North Carolina's largest Civil War battle? See page 15 for the answer.

What is the furniture capital of the world? Look on page 19 for the answer.

Where was actor Andy Griffith born? Page 22 has the answer.

Why is North Carolina called the Tar Heel State? Turn to page 24 for the answer.

Which U.S. president was born in Raleigh? Look on page 31 and find out!

What is NASQUACK? Turn to page 32 for the answer.

That was a great trip! We have traveled all over North Carolina! There are a few places that we didn't have time for, though. Next time, we plan to visit the Shangri-La stone village in Prospect Hill. Visitors to the town can view the collection of 27 miniature buildings there. Tobacco farmer Henry L. Warren began building Shangri-La in 1968.

More Places to Visit in North Carolina

WORDS TO KNOW

aviation (ay-vee-AY-shuhn) constructing and flying airplanes

blowgun (BLOH-guhn) a long, hollow tube through which a sharp object is blown

colony (KOL-uh-nee) a new land settled by people from another country

enchanted (en-CHAN-tid) magical or charming

industries (IN-duh-streez) types of businesses

lighthouses (LITE-houss-ez) tall, thin buildings with a bright light on top to warn ships that they are near shore

resident (REZ-uh-duhnt) someone or something living in a certain place

static electricity (STAT-ik i-lek-TRISS-uh-tee) electrical energy produced by rubbing two objects together

traditions (truh-DISH-uhnz) customs handed down over many years

North Carolina covers 48,711 square miles (126,161 sq km). It's the 29th-largest state in size.

STATE SYMBOLS

State beverage: Milk
State bird: Cardinal
State blue berry: Blueberry
State boat: Shad boat
State colors: Red and blue
State dog: Plott hound
State fish: Channel bass
State flower: Flowering dogwood
State fruit: Scuppernong grape
State insect: Honeybee
State mammal: Gray squirrel
State precious stone: Emerald
State red berry: Strawberry
State reptile: Eastern box turtle
State rock: Granite
State shell: Scotch bonnet
State toast: "The Tar Heel Toast"
State tree: Pine
State vegetable: Sweet potato

State flag

State seal

STATE SONG

"The Old North State"

Words by William Gaston; music by Mrs. E. E. Randolph

Carolina! Carolina! Heaven's blessings attend her,
While we live we will cherish, protect and defend her,
Tho' the scorner may sneer at and witlings defame her,
Still our hearts swell with gladness whenever we name her.
Hurrah! Hurrah! The Old North State forever,
Hurrah! Hurrah! The good Old North State.

Tho' she envies not others, their merited glory,
Say whose name stands the foremost, in liberty's story,
Tho' too true to herself e'er to crouch to oppression,
Who can yield to just rule a more loyal submission.
Hurrah! Hurrah! The Old North State forever,
Hurrah! Hurrah! The good Old North State.

Then let all those who love us, love the land that we live in,
As happy a region as on this side of heaven,
Where plenty and peace, love and joy smile before us,
Raise aloud, raise together the heart-thrilling chorus.
Hurrah! Hurrah! The Old North State forever,
Hurrah! Hurrah! The good Old North State.

FAMOUS PEOPLE

Angelou, Maya (1928–), poet

Byrd, Robert C. (1917–), senator

Junaluska (ca. 1770–1868), Cherokee Indian chief

Coltrane, John (1926–1967), jazz musician

DeMille, Cecil B. (1881–1959), film director

Dole, Elizabeth (1936–), senator

Gardner, Ava (1922–1990), actor

Griffith, Andy (1926–), actor

Graham, Billy (1918–), evangelist

Jackson, Andrew (1767–1845), 7th U.S. president

Johnson, Andrew (1808–1875), 17th U.S. president

Jones, Marion (1975–), Olympic track and field winner

Jordan, Michael (1963–), basketball player

Kuralt, Charles (1934–1997), TV show correspondent and host

Leonard, Sugar Ray (1956–), boxer

Madison, Dolley (1768–1849), first lady

Monk, Thelonious (1917–1982), jazz musician

Polk, James K. (1795–1849), 11th U.S. president

Porter, William Sydney (O. Henry) (1862–1910), author

Scruggs, Earl (1924–), bluegrass musician

Simone, Nina (1933–2003), singer

TO FIND OUT MORE

At the Library
Alex, Nan. *North Carolina*. New York: Children's Press, 2001.

Crane, Carol, and Gary Palmer (illustrator). *T Is for Tar Heel: A North Carolina Alphabet*. Chelsea, Mich.: Sleeping Bear Press, 2003.

Pinkney, Gloria Jean, and Jerry Pinkney (illustrator). *Back Home*. New York: Dial Books for Young Readers, 1992.

Shea, George, and Dan Bolognese (illustrator). *First Flight: The Story of Tom Tate and the Wright Brothers*. New York: HarperCollins Publishers, 1997.

On the Web
Visit our home page for lots of links about North Carolina: *http://www.childsworld.com/links*

Note to Parents, Teachers, and Librarians: We routinely verify our Web links to make sure they are safe, active sites—so encourage your readers to check them out!

Places to Visit or Contact
North Carolina Department of Commerce, Division of Tourism
301 North Wilmington Street
Raleigh, NC 27601
800/847-4862
For more information about traveling in North Carolina

North Carolina Museum of History
4650 Mail Service Center
Raleigh, NC 27699-4650
919/807-7900
For more information about the history of North Carolina

INDEX

Bye, Old North State.
We had a great time.
We'll come back soon!